A
is for Avocet
by
Scott Partridge

A is for Avocet.

B

is for Bunting.

C

is a Curlew, fishing for something.

D

is for Dodo.

E is for Erne.

F

is for Fernwrens, hiding in ferns.

G is for Grebes.

H

is for Hoopoe.

I is an Ibis,
with a long, red nose.

J is for Jay.

K

is for Kite.

L is a Loon calling at night.

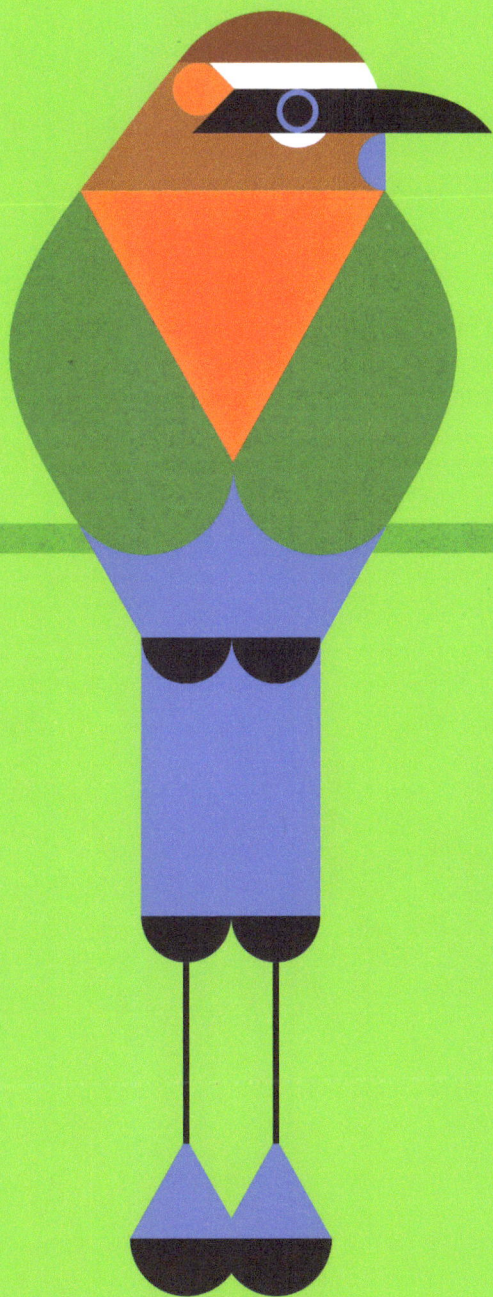

M
is for Motmot.

N

is for Nightjar.

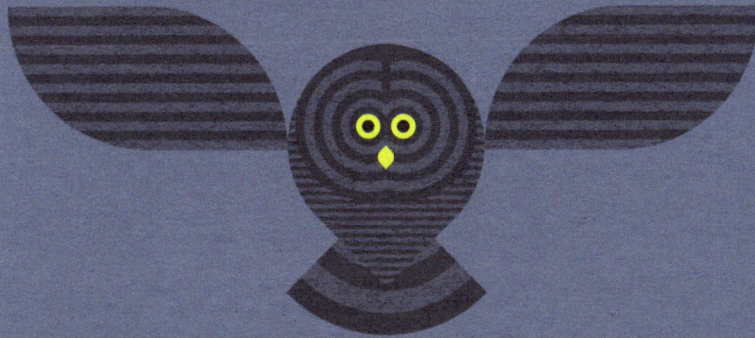

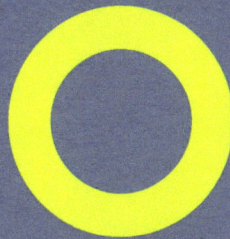

is an Owl,
seen from afar.

P

is for Peewit.

Q

is for Quail.

R
is a Rail,
with a short
stubby tail.

S is for Spoonbill.

T is for Touraco.

U

is an Umbrella Bird,
which looks just like so.

V is for Vulture.

W is for Wren.

X

is a Xenops, which is
seen now and then.

Y

is for Yellowhammer.

z
is for Zebra Dove.

And there are many more, too,
below and above.

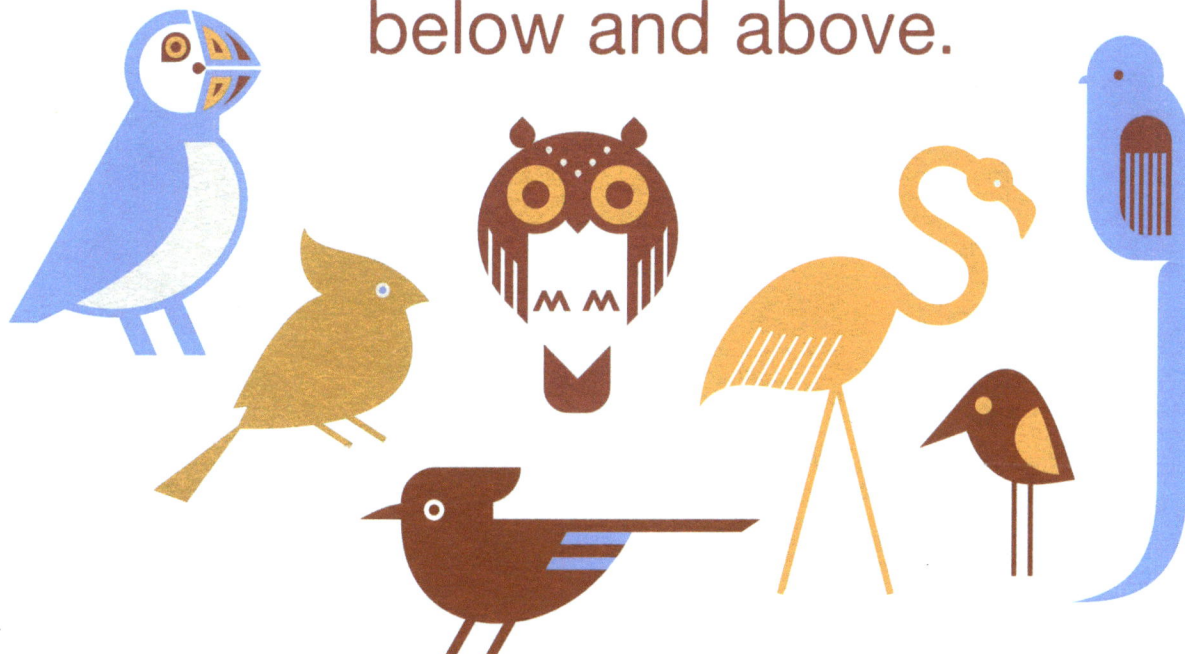

www.ingramcontent.com/pod-product-compliance
Lightning Source LLC
Chambersburg PA
CBHW041539260326
41914CB00015B/1498